DISCOVER!

CALLING ALL COMMUNITY HEROES!

WHO DOES SEARCH AND RESCUE?

BY THERESA EMMINIZER

Enslow PUBLISHING

Please visit our website, www.enslow.com.
For a free color catalog of all our high-quality books, call toll free
1-800-398-2504 or fax 1-877-980-4454.

Cataloging-in-Publication Data
Names: Emminizer, Theresa.
Title: Who does search and rescue? / Theresa Emminizer.
Description: Buffalo, NY : Enslow Publishing, 2025. | Series: Calling all community heroes! | Includes glossary and index.
Identifiers: ISBN 9781978542181 (pbk.) | ISBN 9781978542198 (library bound) | ISBN 9781978542204 (ebook)
Subjects: LCSH: Search and rescue operations–Juvenile literature. | Rescue work–Juvenile literature. |
First responders–Juvenile literature.
Classification: LCC TL553.8 E495 2025 | DDC 363.34'81–dc23

Published in 2025 by
Enslow Publishing
2544 Clinton Street
Buffalo, NY 14224

Designer: Tanya Dellaccio Keeney
Editor: Theresa Emminizer

Photo credits: Cover (background) ASTA DESIGN/Shutterstock.com; cover (speech bubble) mejorana/Shutterstock.com; cover (person) Nasrul Ma Arif/Shutterstock.com; cover (helicopter) Gail Johnson/Shutterstock.com; p. 5 EB Adventure Photography/Shutterstock.com; p. 7 Eric Glenn/Shutterstock.com; p. 9 astarot/Shutterstock.com; p. 11 hxdbzxy/Shutterstock.com; p. 13 Daniel Chetroni/Shutterstock.com; p. 15 jasomtomo/Shutterstock.com; p. 17 Paramarta Bari/Shutterstock.com; p. 19 Steven Matto/Shutterstock.com; p. 21 Prometheus72/Shutterstock.com.

Printed in the United States of America

CPSIA compliance information: Batch #CWENS25: For further information contact Enslow Publishing, at 1-800-398-2504.

CONTENTS

BOLDFACE WORDS APPEAR IN WORDS TO KNOW.

WHAT'S SEARCH AND RESCUE?

Search and Rescue (SAR) is the act of looking for and helping people who are in danger. There are many different situations, or times, in which SAR is used. What's common among them is the goal of finding and aiding missing people.

SEARCH AND RESCUE JOBS ARE CALLED MISSIONS.

WHEN IS IT DONE?

There are different fields of SAR depending on the situation and where help is needed. SAR fields include:

- mountain
- ground
- urban (city)
- air-sea
- combat (military fighting)

The SAR team is based on the field.

A MEMBER OF THE U.S. COAST GUARD SHOWS HOW AN SAR TEAM DROPS FROM A **HELICOPTER** IN A MARITIME, OR OCEAN, MISSION.

WHO DOES IT?

SAR is done by different kinds of workers, including the armed forces, police, firefighters, **medical** workers, national park workers, and **volunteers**. These workers have different training and skills. Often, different kinds of SAR teams work together as partners on a mission.

SAR TEAMS ARE COMMUNITY HEROES!

DISASTER SAR

A natural disaster is a large, harmful event such as a **hurricane**. Local, or nearby, and state SAR teams work with the U.S. government to handle natural disasters. In 2005, Hurricane Katrina hit the Gulf Coast, including Louisiana. Teams from the National Urban Search and Rescue team headed there to help.

AFTER A DISASTER, URBAN SAR TEAMS SEARCH UNDER THE WRECKAGE FOR PEOPLE WHO MAY BE TRAPPED OR HURT.

WILDERNESS SAR

Ground, mountain, and cave SAR teams often work in the **wilderness**. They search for missing hikers and climbers. Wilderness tracking has to do with finding out where the person was last seen, what direction they were going in, and making a search pattern to cover ground.

THIS MOUNTAIN RESCUE TEAM IS SEARCHING FOR A LOST HIKER.

K-9 SAR

SAR dogs are often called K-9s. Dogs have powerful noses that can sniff out certain scents, or smells. That makes them an important part of an SAR team! They go through special training and testing that can take up to two years to finish.

SAR DOGS CAN TRACK ON LAND, IN WATER, AND IN DEEP SNOW.

AN SAR TOOLKIT

An SAR toolkit often has maps and other **navigation** devices, or tools. FINDER is a tool that uses **radar** to pick up heartbeats and tiny movements. It's used to find people deep under building wreckage. SAR teams also need ropes, **harnesses**, and medical tools.

THIS SAR TEAM IS USING ROPES AND PULLEYS TO CARRY A HURT PERSON OUT OF DANGER.

SPECIAL SKILLS

SAR teams work at all hours of the day and night, in all weather, and in dangerous, or unsafe, places. SAR teams need to be strong, decisive, and quick thinkers. They need to know how to track, do rope rescues, treat **injuries**, and more.

SAR TEAMS PRACTICE RESPONDING TO MANY SITUATIONS. THEY ARE TRAINED TO ACT QUICKLY.

SAVING THE DAY

During disasters, SAR teams move in to dig people out. When hikers go missing in the wilderness, SAR teams track them and bring them to safety. Working in caves, mountains, oceans, forests, and cities, SAR teams face many dangers to help people.

THANK YOU, SAR HEROES!

WORDS TO KNOW

harness: A set of straps fitted to a person to keep them in place.

helicopter: An aircraft that has metal blades that spin around its top.

hurricane: A powerful storm that forms over water and causes heavy rainfall and high winds.

injury: Harm or damage.

medical: Having to do with care given by doctors.

navigation: The science of plotting and following a path from one place to another.

radar: A way of using radio waves to find distant objects.

volunteer: A person who works without being paid.

wilderness: A forest or wild place.

wreckage: The broken pieces left after something has been damaged.

FOR MORE INFORMATION

BOOKS

Jones, Dale. *Search and Rescue Dogs*. Minneapolis, MN: Bearport Publishing, 2022.

Laughlin, Kara L. *Search and Rescue Teams on the Scene*. Mankato, MN: The Child's World, 2022.

WEBSITES

FEMA
www.fema.gov/emergency-managers/national-preparedness/frameworks/urban-search-rescue
Learn how the Federal Emergency Management Agency responds to disasters.

National Association for Search and Rescue
nasar.org
Find out more about SAR education and training.

Publisher's note to educators and parents: Our editors have carefully reviewed these websites to ensure that they are suitable for students. Many websites change frequently, however, and we cannot guarantee that a site's future contents will continue to meet our high standards of quality and educational value. Be advised that students should be closely supervised whenever they access the internet.

INDEX